Disney Villains Cookbook

RECIPES
Joy Howard, with additional recipes by Deanna F. Cook
and Cynthia Littlefield

PHOTOGRAPHY
Joe St. Pierre

FOOD STYLING
Joy Howard

ILLUSTRATIONS
The Disney Storybook Art Team

DESIGN
Megan Youngquist

Published by Scholastic Australia in 2025.

Scholastic Australia Pty Limited
PO Box 579 Gosford NSW 2250
ABN 11 000 614 577
www.scholastic.com.au

Part of the Scholastic Group Sydney • Auckland • New York • Toronto • London • Mexico City
New Delhi • Hong Kong • Buenos Aires • Puerto Rico

ISBN 978-1-76172-147-2

Printed in China.

Scholastic Australia's policy, in association with its printers, is to use papers that are renewable and made efficiently with wood from responsibly managed sources, so as to minimise its environmental impact.

Cookbook

SCHOLASTIC
SYDNEY AUCKLAND NEW YORK TORONTO LONDON MEXICO CITY
NEW DELHI HONG KONG BUENOS AIRES PUERTO RICO

Contents

Basics

No-one makes mischief quite like a Disney Villain! Whether it's the Queen's poison apple or Yzma's shape-shifting potions, Ursula's bubbling undersea cauldron full of spells or King Candy's deceptively delicious domain in *Sugar Rush*, the villains know how to wreak havoc—especially by creating mysterious concoctions. Perhaps aspiring chefs can learn a thing or two from their skillful brewing . . . but cooking doesn't have to be villainous! This cookbook is your guide to using the villains' secrets to create scrumptious confections that will satisfy even the muscular Gaston's appetite.

Turn the pages to discover fifty villain-inspired recipes—from breakfast, lunch and dinner, to beverages, sides, snacks and desserts. The recipes are rated on a five 🍎 scale, so if you're a beginner, don't worry! Start with an easier dish (🍎) and work your way up to the more complicated recipes (🍎 🍎 🍎 🍎 🍎).

Now put on your best villainous disguise and get ready to make some delicious treats that are so wickedly good, they might just cast some magic on you!

Before You Begin

Cooking is a lot of fun, but before you get started, there are some important things to remember. Always, always ask a parent for permission. Even the villains need help from their trusty sidekicks to brew their concoctions successfully. If you need to use a stove, oven, blender or mixer for a recipe, make sure to ask an adult to help you. Here are a few other tips to keep in mind.

- If you have long hair, tie it back. You don't want it to end up in the food or near a hot stove.
- Make sure your clothing isn't loose enough to touch a stovetop burner. If you're wearing long sleeves, push them up to your elbows.
- Put on an apron to keep your outfit from getting stained.
- Wash your hands with water and soap for at least twenty seconds so they will be clean when you handle the ingredients.
- Take a few minutes to read the whole recipe so that nothing will come as a surprise once you get started.
- Gather all the equipment you'll need, such as measuring spoons, bowls, baking pans and utensils, before you get out the ingredients.

Measuring Ingredients

To make sure a recipe turns out just the way it's supposed to, you need to measure ingredients exactly. Here are some helpful hints and tips.

- For liquids like milk, water or oil, use a measuring cup with a spout designed for pouring.
- A dry ingredient, such as flour, sugar or cocoa, should be spooned into a measuring cup without a spout. Then, to check that you have the exact amount, scrape the flat edge of a butter knife across the rim of the cup to remove any extra.
- A chunky ingredient should be spooned into a measuring cup and then patted gently, just enough to even out the top without packing it down. Shredded ingredients are also measured this way.
- Brown sugar should be packed into a measuring cup to press out any air bubbles.
- Measuring butter is really easy if you use sticks that have tablespoon marks printed on the wrapper. All you have to do is slice the butter where the line is.

Safety First!

Even when they're getting up to a little villainy, a good cook never forgets that safety always comes first in the kitchen. Here are some important rules to follow.

Using knives, peelers, graters and small kitchen appliances

- Never use a kitchen appliance or sharp utensil without asking an adult for help.
- Always use a cutting board when slicing or chopping ingredients. Grip the knife handle firmly, holding it so that the sharp edge is facing downwards. Then slice through the ingredient, moving the knife away from yourself.
- After slicing raw meat or fish, wash the knife (with an adult's help) as well as the cutting board. You should also wash your hands with water and soap for at least twenty seconds before working with other ingredients.
- If you drop a knife, don't try to catch it. Instead, quickly step back and let the knife fall to the countertop or floor before picking it up by the handle.
- When using a vegetable peeler, press the edge of the blade into the vegetable's skin and then push the peeler away from yourself. Keep in mind that the more pressure you use, the thicker the peeling will be.
- Use electrical appliances, such as mixers and blenders, in a cleared space far away from the sink and other wet areas. And always unplug a mixer or blender before scraping a mixture from the beaters or blades.

Working around hot things

- Always ask an adult for help around a hot stovetop or oven.
- Make sure to point the handle of a stovetop pan away from you so you won't knock into it and accidentally tip the pot over.
- Use pot holders or oven mitts every time you touch a stovetop pot or skillet—even if it's just the lid. You should also use pot holders whenever you put a pan in the oven or take it out.
- Remember, steam can burn! Be sure to step back a bit when straining hot foods, such as pasta or cooked vegetables.
- Don't forget to shut off the oven or stove when the food is done baking or cooking.

Preparing Fruits and Vegetables

It's important to wash produce before adding it to a recipe. Here are some tips for making sure fruits and vegetables are clean and ready to use.

- Rinse produce well under plain running water. Don't use soap! If the produce is firm, like an apple or carrot, rub the surface to help remove any garden soil or grit. You can put softer fruits and vegetables, such as berries and broccoli florets, in a small colander or strainer before rinsing.
- Use a vegetable brush to scrub vegetables that grow underground, like potatoes and carrots. You should also scrub any fruits and vegetables that grow right on the ground, such as cucumbers and melons.
- Dry the washed produce with a paper towel or reusable cleaning cloth and cut off any bruised parts before using it in a recipe.

Cleaning Up

A good cook always leaves the kitchen as tidy as they found it. This means cleaning all the bowls, pots, pans and utensils you used to prepare the recipe. Here are some tips for making sure everything is spick-and-span.

- Always ask an adult for help washing knives and appliances with sharp blades, such as a blender or food processor.
- As you cook, try to give each bowl and utensil a quick rinse as soon as you're done with it. That way leftover food or batter won't stick to it before you can wash it with soap and water.
- Put all the ingredients back where they belong so you'll know just where to find them the next time you cook.
- Wipe down your work area—including the countertop and sink—with a damp paper towel or reusable cleaning cloth.
- Double-check that all the appliances you used are turned off before you leave the kitchen.
- Hang up your apron, or put it in the laundry if it needs to be washed.

Breakfast

Makes 8

Ingredients

½ cup apple juice

1 frozen banana

1 cup frozen mango

4 ice cubes

Toppings

Sliced strawberries and blueberries

Half an apple

Tip

If you'd prefer, you can slice up the apple at the centre of the smoothie to make it easier to eat—or try another fruity topping!

The Queen's Bewitching Apple Bowl

The Queen is quite the expert when it comes to apples! This simple smoothie bowl recipe will have you making your own magic with apples in no time.

Directions

1. Ask an adult for help with the blender. Place the apple juice, frozen banana, frozen mango and ice cubes into the blender.
2. Blend the ingredients until they are smooth and creamy.
3. Pour the smoothie into a bowl, add your preferred toppings, and serve with a spoon.

Spotted Scones

The fashion-obsessed Cruella is best known for her fixation on fabulous spotted clothes, but she'd likely devour a batch of these polka-dot delights too. They're flavoured with orange zest and chocolate chips, and topped with sugar.

Makes 8

Ingredients

2 cups flour, plus more for dusting

3 Tbsp sugar

½ tsp kosher salt

2 tsp baking powder

¾ tsp orange zest

½ cup chocolate chips

½ cup (1 stick) cold unsalted butter

2 eggs

1¼ tsp vanilla extract

125 ml full-cream milk

125 ml thickened cream

Sugar to sprinkle

Directions

1. Line a baking sheet with baking paper. In a large bowl, whisk together the flour, sugar, salt, baking powder, orange zest and chocolate chips. With an adult's help, use a box grater to grate the butter into the flour mixture. Use your hands to toss the butter into the flour a few times.

2. In another bowl, whisk together 1 egg, the vanilla, the full-cream milk and the thickened cream. Combine the two mixtures and blend until the flour is moistened. Do not overmix.

3. Turn the dough out onto a lightly floured surface. Pat it into a 1.5 cm-thick circle and cut into 8 even wedges. Place the scones on the prepared baking sheet, then refrigerate while the oven heats.

4. Ask an adult for help with the oven. Heat the oven to 200°C. Whisk together the remaining egg with 1 tablespoon water. Brush the top of each scone with the egg wash and sprinkle generously with sugar. Bake the scones until golden brown on the top and bottom, about 20 minutes, rotating the pan halfway through.

Makes 8

Ingredients

1 (35 cm) half baguette

4 eggs

3 Tbsp heavy cream

¼ tsp kosher salt

Black pepper

⅓ cup shredded cheddar

1 spring onion, chopped

2 strips cooked bacon, roughly chopped

Tip

Check out page 130 *for a step-by-step guide on how to trim the baguette so you can fill it with the egg mixture.*

Baguette Breakfast Beaks

This dish, featuring eggs baked right into a loaf of toasty bread, is sliced into wedges shaped like a bird's beak as a nod to the winged accomplices Iago and the Raven. Perch them on a plate for your next weekend brunch and watch every slice fly away!

Directions

1. Ask an adult for help with the oven. Heat the oven to 175°C. Have an adult use a sharp knife to cut a rectangle out of the baguette, being careful not to cut through the sides or bottom. Place the loaf on a baking sheet.
2. In a large liquid measuring cup, whisk together the eggs, heavy cream, salt and a few grinds of pepper. Stir in the cheddar, spring onion and bacon. Carefully pour the mixture into the baguette (you may have a little left over).
3. Bake until the egg is puffy and set, about 25 minutes. Let sit for 5 minutes, then slice into 8 even wedges. Serve immediately.

Rosy Red Porridge

The cantankerous Queen of Hearts is not easy to please, though given her affinity for red, she might approve of a breakfast like this rose-tinted bowl. Fresh strawberries give the bowl its blushing hue and are also sliced, shaped into hearts, and scattered on top.

Serves 2

Ingredients

1½ cups oat milk

1½ cups strawberries, trimmed and halved, plus 2 more for slicing

1 cup quick oats

Kosher salt

2 Tbsp maple syrup

Directions

1. In a blender, pulse the milk and strawberries until the berries are in small chunks.
2. Ask an adult for help at the stove. Place the mixture in a medium saucepan. Bring to a boil.
3. Add the oats and a pinch of salt. Reduce the heat to low and cook until done, about 5 minutes. Add the maple syrup. Let cool slightly.
4. While the porridge cools, slice each remaining berry. Trim the tops of each slice to form a heart shape. Evenly divide the porridge between two bowls, then top each portion with strawberry hearts. Serve immediately.

Tip

Make this porridge your own by experimenting with other toppings like nuts, fruit and more.

Serves 8

Ingredients

12 large eggs

½ cup heavy cream

¾ tsp kosher salt

½ tsp black pepper

1 Tbsp olive oil

125 g Swiss brown mushrooms, sliced

2 spring onions, sliced, whites and greens separated

2 cups fresh baby spinach, roughly chopped

1½ cups shredded cheddar

Tip

Once you learn how to make the frittata base, you can play around with what types of cheese, veggies or other toppings to add to the mix!

Dozen-Egg Frittata

Gaston claims to eat five dozen eggs a day to maintain his muscular figure. You need only one dozen eggs to make this dish, but there will still be plenty for a crowd. An added bonus: there's spinach, mushrooms and cheddar tucked into every bite.

Directions

1. Ask an adult for help with the oven. Heat the oven to 200°C. In a medium bowl, whisk together the eggs, heavy cream, salt and pepper. Set aside.
2. Ask an adult for help at the stove. In a 25.4 cm cast-iron skillet over medium heat, warm the oil. Add the mushrooms and white part of the spring onion and cook until the mushrooms and spring onions have softened, about 5 minutes. Stir in the spinach and spring onion greens and cook until wilted, about 2 minutes.
3. Set aside a few tablespoons of the cheese. Add the egg mixture and remaining cheese to the skillet and stir to combine. Top with the reserved cheese.
4. Reduce the heat to medium low and continue to cook undisturbed until it begins to set around the edges, about 5 minutes. With an adult's help, place the skillet in the oven and bake until set, about 10 to 15 minutes more. Let cool for a few minutes before slicing and serving.

Blackberry French Toast Casserole

Dark berries and spices conjure a wickedly tasty breakfast that rivals any spell Maleficent could cast. Letting this dish rest for a while after it comes out of the oven gives it more time to set and makes it even more delicious.

Directions

1. Ask an adult for help with the oven. Heat the oven to 160°C. Spread the bread on a baking sheet and bake until dried out but not browned, about 15 minutes, turning halfway through. Let cool on the pan, then transfer to a large bowl.
2. Butter a 20 cm baking dish. In a medium bowl, whisk together the egg yolks and sugar. Add the thickened cream and the full-cream milk, vanilla, salt, cinnamon and nutmeg and whisk until evenly blended. Pour the mixture over the bread and gently toss to evenly moisten the bread.
3. Cover the bottom of the baking dish with half the bread cubes. Sprinkle on half the berries. Repeat with the other halves of the bread cubes and berries. Pour any remaining egg mixture over the bread and berries, cover the casserole and refrigerate for 30 minutes.
4. Bake the dish until the casserole is set in the centre, about 1 hour, rotating the pan halfway through. Let the casserole rest for at least 15 minutes and dust with icing sugar, if using, before serving.

Serves 9

Ingredients

¾ loaf challah bread, diced into 2.5 cm cubes (8 cups)

Butter, for greasing

4 egg yolks

½ cup sugar

375 ml thickened cream

375 ml full-cream milk

1¾ tsp vanilla extract

¼ tsp kosher salt

1¼ tsp ground cinnamon

¼ tsp ground nutmeg

2 cups blackberries

Icing sugar, for dusting (optional)

Tip

Not sure how to separate egg yolks from the rest of the egg? ***Check out the Glossary on page 140!***

Lunch

Kronk's Spinach Puffs

Makes 9

Yzma's faithful sidekick, Kronk, is a talented chef, and spinach puffs are one of his specialties. Make this recipe your own 'new groove'!

Ingredients

450 g frozen spinach, thawed and squeezed

4 spring onions, chopped

⅓ cup crumbled feta

⅓ cup cottage cheese

2 Tbsp shredded Parmesan

3 eggs

¾ tsp kosher salt

⅛ tsp white pepper

2 sheets frozen puff pastry from a 500 g package, thawed

Directions

1. Ask an adult for help with the oven. Heat the oven to 200°C. Use a sieve or cheesecloth to squeeze and drain the water from the spinach. Place in a medium bowl with the spring onions, feta, cottage cheese, Parmesan, 2 eggs and salt and pepper. Stir to combine.
2. Ask an adult for help with knives. Evenly cut each pastry sheet into 9 squares. Press each dough portion into the well of a standard cupcake pan, letting the corners hang over the edges. Spoon a generous tablespoon of the spinach mixture into each pastry.
3. Gather the corners of each dough square and pinch them closed. In a small bowl, whisk together the remaining egg with 1 tablespoon water. Brush the tops of the pastries with this egg wash. Bake until golden and crisp, about 25 minutes. Let cool slightly before serving.

Tip

If you use the microwave or stovetop to thaw your spinach, be sure to let the spinach cool completely. Using it while still hot could cause the eggs to start cooking too quickly.

Makes 8

Ingredients

2½ cups chopped rotisserie chicken

⅓ cup mayonnaise

2 Tbsp chopped roasted red capsicum

1 large stalk celery, sliced

1 Tbsp chopped chives, plus more for garnish

¼ cup chopped smoked almonds

¼ tsp smoked paprika, plus more for garnish

Black pepper

1 small head oak leaf lettuce

Tip

As an alternative to using a sharp knife, you can snip the celery, capsicum and chives with kitchen scissors.

Smoky Chicken Salad Cups

Hades, the god of the Underworld, is known for his ability to create flames. While not as fiery as some of his creations, this chicken salad still has a bit of smolder: both the almonds and paprika are the smoked variety, which gives the lettuce cups a unique flavour.

Directions

1. In a large bowl, stir together the chicken, mayonnaise, capsicum, celery, chives, almonds and paprika. Season lightly with black pepper, then taste, and adjust seasoning if needed.
2. Tear 8 leaves from the head of lettuce. Fill each with ⅓ cup of the salad. Serve immediately.

Mini Tamatoa Seaweed Rolls

A batch of these hand rolls will attract hungry friends, just as Tamatoa's shiny shell draws in curious fish. Ask an adult to help you prep the vegetables, and don't worry too much about the look of the end result. It will be tasty no matter what!

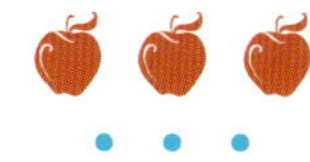

Makes 8

Ingredients

¾ cup uncooked sushi rice

2 Tbsp rice vinegar

1½ tsp sugar

¼ tsp kosher salt

1 tsp black sesame seeds

4 large sheets nori, halved crosswise

1 large carrot, cut into matchsticks

1–2 Lebanese cucumbers, cut into matchsticks

1 large avocado, sliced

Soy sauce, for dipping

Directions

1. Cook the rice according to the package directions.
2. Meanwhile, in a small bowl, stir together the vinegar, sugar and salt until the latter two are dissolved. Pour the mixture over the rice, add the sesame seeds, and stir to coat evenly. Let the rice mixture cool completely.
3. Spread a heaping ¼ cup of rice on a nori sheet. Arrange one-eighth of the carrot, cucumber and avocado in the centre of the sheet (vegetables can be trimmed if they are too long). Roll into a cone or log, as shown (see page 131). Repeat with the remaining nori, rice and vegetables. Serve immediately with soy sauce.

Tip

Check out page 131 *for a step-by-step guide on how to create these seaweed rolls!*

Makes 6

Ingredients

Flour, for dusting

1 (23 cm) refrigerated piecrust

2 Tbsp pizza sauce

10 pepperoni slices, roughly chopped

½ cup shredded mozzarella

1 large egg

12 black olives

Tip

It's tempting to stack these pockets extra high with fillings, but try to use filling sparingly. Using less will make it easier to form the all-important lion's mane.

Roaring Pizza Pockets

Want to take 'pride' in your lunch? Try making these Scar-shaped pockets that combine the delicious flavours of pepperoni pizza with buttery pie crust.

Directions

1. Ask an adult for help with the oven. Heat the oven to 200°C and line a baking sheet with baking paper. On a lightly floured surface, roll out the piecrust to a 33 cm circle. Use a 6 cm round cutter to shape 12 circles from the dough, gathering and rerolling the dough as needed.
2. Arrange half the dough rounds on the prepared baking sheet. Top each with 1 teaspoon sauce, leaving a 2.5 cm border. Add ⅙ of the chopped pepperoni slices and a heaping tablespoon mozzarella to each. (You will have some cheese left over.)
3. Whisk the egg in a small bowl with 1 tablespoon water. Brush the edges of each filling-topped dough round with the egg wash, then top each with one of the remaining dough rounds. Use a fork to crimp the edges of each pocket, then brush their tops with the egg wash. Trim the olives into 12 eyes and 6 noses. Add a set to each pocket, then add cheese whiskers, as shown.
4. Bake the pockets until golden brown, about 15 minutes. Serve immediately.

Playing-Card Sandwiches

These teensy sandwiches filled with hummus and cucumber are suited just like the Queen of Hearts' loyal playing-card soldiers. But you can change up what's inside each bite any way you wish (just as the Queen would surely do!). Switch up the vegetables or sandwich spread, or swap them both for cream cheese and jam.

Makes 8

Ingredients

4 slices of your favourite sandwich bread

6 Tbsp hummus

12 thin slices cucumber

Directions

1. Spread one side of each bread slice with the hummus. Arrange the cucumbers on half the bread slices, then top each with a remaining slice, hummus side down.
2. Use mini diamond, heart, club and spade cookie cutters to cut small shapes from each sandwich. Discard the scraps and serve.

Tip

Be sure to slice the cucumber extra thin so it will be easier to cut through with the cookie cutters.

Serves about 10

Ingredients

1 Tbsp olive oil

1 Tbsp butter

1 large onion

2 medium carrots, chopped

2 stalks celery, chopped

2 garlic cloves, minced

1 tsp grated fresh ginger

½ tsp ground cumin

1 tsp kosher salt

½ tsp black pepper

About 6 cups butternut squash, chopped

2 medium apples, peeled and chopped

4 cups chicken broth

Tip

Enjoy this soup topped with croutons or with a slice of bread for sopping up the last drop.

Golden Squash and Apple Soup

The Queen used an apple to cast a spell, but the fruit in this recipe supplies nothing more than a touch of sweetness to an already yummy golden soup.

Directions

1. Ask an adult for help at the stove. In a large pot over medium heat, melt the oil and butter. Add the onion, carrots and celery, and cook until softened, about 8 minutes. Add the garlic, ginger, cumin, salt and pepper and cook 1 minute. Stir in the squash and apples, then add the broth.
2. Bring the mixture to a boil. Once boiling, reduce to a simmer, then let cook until the vegetables are completely softened, about 12 minutes.
3. With an adult's help, use a blender to puree the soup in batches—be careful; the soup will be very hot! Serve immediately.

Lady Tremaine's Emerald Grain Bowl

Lady Tremaine isn't known for her kindness, but this grain bowl made with vegetables and brown rice is as wholesome as can be. The broccoli, green beans, cucumbers, edamame and herby avocado dressing in the bowl resemble Lady Tremaine's emerald green jewels.

Serves 4

Ingredients

250 g green beans, ends removed

1 medium crown broccoli, cut into florets

1 Tbsp olive oil

Kosher salt

Black pepper

1 avocado, roughly chopped

1 garlic clove, grated

2 Tbsp lime juice

½ cup packed fresh coriander

2 tsp honey

2 cups cooked brown rice, warmed

½ cup frozen edamame, thawed

2 Lebanese cucumbers, sliced

Directions

1. Ask an adult for help with the oven. Heat the oven to 230°C. On a large sheet pan, toss the green beans and broccoli with the olive oil. Roast until slightly charred and tender, about 12 minutes. Season with salt and pepper to taste.
2. While the vegetables cook, make the dressing. Use a blender to puree the avocado, garlic, lime juice, coriander, honey and 3 tablespoons water until smooth. Season with salt and pepper to taste and blend once more.
3. Fill a bowl with one-quarter of the rice, then top with one-quarter each of the green bean and broccoli mixture, edamame and cucumber. Top with a spoonful of the dressing. Serve immediately.

Serves 4

Ingredients

Muffuletta Spread

1 (155 g) jar pimiento-stuffed green olives, drained and sliced

1 tomato, seeded and chopped

1 clove garlic, minced

1 tsp dried oregano

3 Tbsp olive oil

2 Tbsp balsamic vinegar

½ tsp ground black pepper

Sandwich

1 round loaf of Italian bread

Olive oil

100 g each of sliced deli ham, salami, provolone cheese and Monterey Jack or swiss cheese

Muffuletta Sandwich

Dr. Facilier makes his mischief in the city of New Orleans, where this popular sandwich is all the rage.

Directions

1. Combine all the muffuletta spread ingredients in a bowl and stir until well mixed.
2. Slice the bread loaf in half lengthwise. Brush or drizzle the bottom piece with olive oil.
3. Layer on the meats, the cheeses and the muffuletta spread, and then cover everything with the top half of the bread loaf.
4. Slice the sandwich into four wedges.

Dinner

Captain Hook's Stuffed Shells

Serves 6

After weeks of humble grub while out at sea, Captain Hook and his crew would no doubt appreciate a warm plate of this ocean-themed dish. Each oversized shell is stuffed with a pillowy dollop of ricotta and drenched in a delicious ladling of red sauce.

Ingredients

15 jumbo pasta shells

1 large egg

1¼ cups whole milk ricotta

1 garlic clove, grated

1 Tbsp fresh chopped parsley, plus more for garnish

¾ cup grated mozzarella

2 Tbsp grated Parmesan

½ tsp kosher salt

¼ tsp black pepper

1¼ cups marinara sauce

Directions

1. Ask an adult for help with the oven and stovetop. Heat the oven to 190°C and bring a large pot of water to a boil. Add the pasta to the water and cook according to the package directions.
2. While the pasta cooks, stir together the egg, ricotta, garlic, parsley, ½ cup mozzarella, 1 tablespoon Parmesan, salt and pepper in a medium bowl.
3. Evenly spread ½ cup of the marinara over the bottom of an 20 cm baking dish. Add a spoonful of the ricotta mixture to the centre of a pasta shell. Place the shell in the prepared baking dish. Repeat with the remaining shells and ricotta mixture.
4. Cover the shells with the remaining ¾ cup marinara and sprinkle on the remaining cheese. Cover the dish with foil and bake 30 minutes. Uncover the dish and bake 10 minutes more. Let sit for 5 to 10 minutes before serving.

Tip

*Pair this dish with a vegetable side—like Yzma's Roasted Broccoli with Parmesan on **page 66**.*

Serves 4

Ingredients

1 cup plain yoghurt

2 tsp ground cumin

2 tsp smoked paprika

½ tsp ground coriander

1 tsp lemon zest

2 garlic cloves, grated

600 g chicken breast, cut into 2.5 cm cubes

1 large green capsicum, cut into large pieces

1 large yellow capsicum, cut into large pieces

1 large red onion, cut into large pieces

Tip

Do you know the difference between grilling and baking? ***Check out the Glossary on page 139*** *to find out.*

Spiced Chicken Kebabs

A marinade of yoghurt, spices and lots of lemon and garlic gives these oven-grilled chicken skewers their unique taste. It's a simple dish you can dress up by serving it on a fancy platter—a choice the discerning Jafar would most certainly approve of.

Directions

1. In a small bowl, stir together yoghurt, cumin, paprika, coriander, lemon zest and garlic. Set aside. Line a baking sheet with foil.
2. Ask an adult for help preparing the skewers. Thread the chicken, capsicums and onion onto eight 20 cm skewers in an alternating pattern. Place them on the prepared baking sheet.
3. Brush the skewers on all sides with the yoghurt mixture. Place the pan in the refrigerator and let marinate for at least 1 hour.
4. Ask an adult for help with the oven. Heat the oven to 220°C. Bake the skewers for 15 minutes. Remove from the oven, flip, and set the broiler to high. Broil the skewers until the chicken is cooked through and the vegetables are lightly charred around the edges, about 10 minutes. Serve immediately.

Shape-Shifting Pesto Pasta

If Hades's loyal minions Panic and Pain were to morph into a delicious bowl of pasta, it would probably look a lot like this one with its noodles in many shapes. A bright homemade basil pesto, Italian sausage and fresh tomatoes round out the recipe.

Serves 6

Ingredients

½ cup plus 1 Tbsp olive oil

350 g Italian sausage, casing removed

350 g mixed pasta (such as fusilli, rotelle and rigatoni)

3 cups basil leaves

2 small garlic cloves, roughly chopped

3 Tbsp pine nuts

5 Tbsp Parmesan

1 tsp kosher salt

Black pepper

1 cup cherry tomatoes, halved

Directions

1. Ask an adult for help at the stove. Warm a skillet over medium heat. Add 1 tablespoon oil and heat. Add the sausage and cook, stirring occasionally, until browned. Transfer to a paper towel-lined plate.
2. Bring a large pot of water to a boil. Add the pasta and cook according to the package directions. Drain, reserving ¼ cup of the pasta water.
3. Meanwhile, in a blender or food processor, combine the basil, garlic, pine nuts, Parmesan, salt and a few grinds of pepper. Pulse to chop. With the machine running, add the remaining oil in a slow, steady stream until well blended.
4. In a large bowl, toss together the cooked pasta, sausage, pesto, 2 tablespoons pasta water and tomatoes. Add 1 or 2 tablespoons more of the pasta water if the pasta is dry. Serve immediately.

Tip

This dish is a clever way to use up small amounts of leftover dry pasta. Just be sure the cooking times are similar when you mix and match different shapes.

Serves 6

Ingredients

2 Tbsp vegetable oil

1 small garlic clove, grated

1 tsp grated fresh ginger

1 tsp garam masala

¾ tsp ground cumin

¼ tsp ground turmeric

¾ tsp kosher salt

¼ tsp black pepper

1 small onion, finely chopped

1 small head cauliflower, cut into florets

2 medium white potatoes, diced

3 whole peeled tomatoes (from a 400 g can)

¼ cup chopped coriander

Tip

Enjoy this dish alongside a serving of naan or basmati rice.

Kaa's Aloo Gobi

The always-ravenous Kaa isn't known for eating many vegetables. However, this vegetarian dish of cauliflower, potato and a warm blend of spices just might entice him.

Directions

1. Ask an adult for help at the stove. In a large skillet over medium heat, warm the oil. Add the garlic, ginger, garam masala, cumin, turmeric, salt and pepper. Cook 1 minute. Add the onion and cook until softened, about 3 minutes. Add the cauliflower and potatoes and continue to cook, stirring frequently, until beginning to soften, about 8 minutes. Add the tomatoes, using your hands to break them into small pieces, then stir to combine.
2. Add ⅓ cup water to the pan, cover, and continue to cook until the vegetables are softened, about 10 minutes more. Sprinkle with coriander before serving.

Gaston's Chicken Drumsticks

Makes 8

These drumsticks would fit right in on the menu at Gaston's favourite tavern! They're the perfect dinner to satisfy a hearty appetite.

Ingredients

8 chicken drumsticks

3 Tbsp olive oil

2 garlic cloves, grated

1 tsp lemon zest, plus lemon wedges for serving

2 Tbsp mixed herbs

1½ tsp kosher salt

1 tsp black pepper

Directions

1. Ask an adult for help with the oven. Heat the oven to 220°C. Fit a baking tray with a baking rack.
2. In a large bowl, toss together all the ingredients until the chicken is evenly coated. Arrange the pieces on the rack. Bake until golden and crispy, about 40 minutes. Serve immediately with lemon wedges.

Tip

If you like them extra crispy, you can grill the drumsticks for 2 or 3 minutes after baking. Be sure to watch them carefully so they don't burn.

Serves 4

Ingredients

450 g firm tofu, drained

⅓ cup flour

1½ tsp salt

¾ tsp garlic powder

¾ tsp onion powder

½ tsp paprika

2 Tbsp coconut aminos

1 Tbsp lemon juice

3 Tbsp soy milk

¾ cup panko bread crumbs

1 Tbsp vegetable oil

8 (snack-size) sheets nori, crumbled

Tip

Turn to page 132 *to learn how to cut your tofu sticks evenly without a ruler.*

Fishy Sticks

This recipe may resemble crunchy fish sticks, but it's actually made using tofu. Share these with unsuspecting friends or family and see how they react—a clever ruse not unlike Ursula's disguise as Vanessa, but with a much happier result!

Directions

1. Ask an adult for help with the oven. Heat the oven to 190°C. Line a baking tray with baking paper. Slice the tofu into 12 even pieces.
2. In a shallow bowl, combine the flour, 1 teaspoon salt, garlic powder, onion powder and paprika. In another bowl, stir together the coconut aminos, lemon juice and soy milk. In a third bowl, combine the panko and vegetable oil, then stir in the nori and remaining ½ teaspoon salt.
3. Dredge a tofu piece in the flour. Dip in the soy mixture, then gently toss in the panko mixture to evenly coat. Place on the baking tray. Repeat with the remaining tofu pieces.
4. Bake the tofu for 15 minutes, then flip and bake until golden and crunchy, for about 15 minutes more. Let cool slightly before serving.

Dr. Facilier's Baking Tray Prawn Boil

This New Orleans–inspired seafood boil doesn't use any water! Instead of placing the spicy sausage, prawn and veggies in an oversized pot on the stove, they're spread onto a sheet pan and baked in the oven with the same flavourful, savoury result.

Serves 4

Ingredients

2 tsp Old Bay seasoning

½ to 1 tsp Cajun seasoning

340 g baby red potatoes

3 Tbsp olive oil

2 large ears corn, quartered

340 g smoked andouille (or chorizo)

230 g large prawns, peeled and deveined

Directions

1. Ask an adult for help with the oven. Heat the oven to 220°C. In a small bowl, stir together the Old Bay and Cajun seasoning.
2. Toss the potatoes with one-third of the seasoning mix and 1 tablespoon oil. Spread the potatoes on a baking tray and bake 20 minutes.
3. Toss the corn and andouille with one-third of the seasoning and 1 tablespoon oil. Add the mixture to the sheet pan and bake 10 minutes. Toss the prawns and remaining seasoning mix with 1 tablespoon oil, then add to the same baking tray and bake until the prawns are pink and opaque, about 5 minutes. Serve immediately.

Tip

For a Facilier-themed feast, pair this recipe with the Blueberry Sparkler beverage ***on page 94***.

Serves 6

Ingredients

Breadsticks

350 g to 500 g pizza dough

Flour, for dusting

1 Tbsp peppercorns

Stew

2 Tbsp olive oil

1 (400 g) package chorizo, thinly sliced

1 large onion, chopped

3 garlic cloves, minced

1½ tsp salt

¼ tsp pepper

4 cups chicken broth

3 medium white potatoes, peeled and cut into 2.5 cm cubes

½ large bunch green kale, torn into bite-size pieces (about 6 cups)

1 (400 g) can white beans, rinsed and drained

Serpent Stew

Just like Jafar and his serpent staff, these serpent-shaped breadsticks and stew make a powerful pair.

Directions

1. Ask an adult for help with the oven. Heat the oven to 200°C and line two baking trays with baking paper. Divide the dough into 8 to 10 portions. On a lightly floured surface, roll a portion into a 60 cm-long rope. Working directly on one of the prepared sheets, wind and shape the rope into a snake. Repeat with the remaining dough, spacing each snake 5 cm apart.
2. Press a pair of peppercorn eyes into each snake. Bake the snakes until golden and puffed, about 10 minutes. Set aside to cool.
3. Ask an adult for help at the stove. In a large pot over medium heat, warm the oil. Add the chorizo and cook until browned, about 8 minutes. Transfer the meat to a bowl. Add the onion to the pan and cook until softened, about 3 minutes. Add the garlic and cook for 1 minute. Season with the salt and pepper, then add the broth and 3 cups water, and bring to a boil.
4. Place the potatoes in the pot and reduce the heat to a simmer. Continue to simmer until the potatoes are cooked through, about 12 minutes. Ask an adult for help with the blender. Remove half the stew from the pot and purée it in the blender. Add it back to the pot along with the kale and white beans, and return to a simmer. Cook until the kale is wilted, about 8 minutes. Serve each portion hot in a bowl topped with a snake breadstick.

Sides

Yzma's Roasted Broccoli with Parmesan

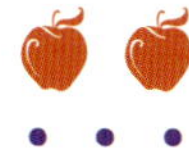

Serves 5

Ingredients

2 medium broccoli crowns (about 680 g), cut into florets

4 tsp olive oil

¼ tsp kosher salt

2 Tbsp grated Parmesan

1 Tbsp lemon juice

When one of Yzma's nefarious plans is foiled, she attempts to signal her sidekick, Kronk, for help using two stalks of broccoli. The florets in this recipe are sprinkled with fresh-squeezed lemon juice and Parmesan cheese—a combination far too tasty to waste on any shenanigans!

Directions

1. Ask an adult for help with the oven. Heat the oven to 240°C. On a large baking tray, toss together the broccoli, olive oil and salt. Roast the broccoli on the bottom rack until crisp, tender and charred in spots, about 12 to 15 minutes, flipping halfway through.
2. With an adult's help, transfer the broccoli to a medium bowl and toss with the Parmesan and lemon juice. Serve immediately.

Tip

If you like, you can use crumbled feta cheese in this recipe in place of Parmesan.

Serves 6

Ingredients

680 g purple potatoes (or a combination of red and purple potatoes)

2 stalks celery, sliced

2 spring onions, sliced

¼ cup mayonnaise

1 tsp Dijon mustard

1 Tbsp apple cider vinegar

¼ tsp kosher salt

¼ tsp black pepper

2 Tbsp olive oil

1 Tbsp chopped fresh dill

Tip

Dill is the perfect complement to this tasty salad, but you can also use parsley or tarragon in its place.

Maleficent's Purple Potato Salad

Whether Maleficent is in human or dragon form, her purple colour scheme is hard to miss. This purple salad has a traditional creamy lemon-and-herb-flavoured dressing, but it's dressed lightly to show off its unique hue.

Directions

1. Ask an adult for help at the stove. Bring a large pot of salted water to a boil. Add the potatoes and cook until tender, about 12 minutes. Drain, then transfer to a large bowl and cool completely. Once cooled, add the celery and spring onions.
2. In a small bowl, combine the mayonnaise, mustard, vinegar, salt, pepper, olive oil and dill. Whisk until well blended, then pour over the potato mixture. Stir to coat the vegetables evenly. Refrigerate until ready to serve.

Black and White Bean Salad

Serves 6

Can you guess which villain is most likely to enjoy this picnic-worthy side complete with two kinds of beans, sweet capsicums and a bright and citrusy homemade dressing? Here's a hint: the main ingredients match the colours of her extraordinary hair.

Ingredients

1 (425 g) can black beans, drained and rinsed

1 (425 g) can cannellini beans, drained and rinsed

½ large red capsicum, chopped

3 Tbsp chopped shallots

2 Tbsp chopped coriander

5 Tbsp olive oil

¾ tsp smoked paprika

3 Tbsp lime juice

¾ tsp kosher salt

¼ tsp black pepper

Directions

1. In a large bowl, combine the beans, capsicum, shallots and coriander.
2. In a small bowl, whisk together the olive oil, paprika, lime juice, salt and pepper.
3. Pour the dressing over the salad and toss to coat the vegetables evenly. Refrigerate until ready to serve.

Tip

This salad comes together quickly, but you can also make it a day ahead if you'd like.

Serves 6

Ingredients

½ of 1 rockmelon
1 small dragon fruit
½ cup blueberries
½ cup raspberries
½ cup green grapes
Juice of ½ lime
1 Tbsp honey
1 small star fruit, sliced (optional)

Tip

If you can't find star fruit, you can substitute your own favourite fruit by cutting it into thick slices, then using a star-shaped food cutter to shape it.

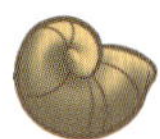

Ursula's Sea Bubble Berry Salad

A melon baller—a small round spoon made for scooping—gives some of the fruit in this rainbow salad a round shape, just like the bubbles swirling around Ursula's ocean lair.

Directions

1. Use a melon baller to scoop the rockmelon and place the fruit in a large bowl. With an adult's help, halve the dragon fruit. Use the melon baller once more to shape the fruit, and add it to the bowl with the rockmelon. Gently toss in the blueberries, raspberries and grapes.
2. In a small bowl, stir together the lime juice and honey. Pour the mixture over the fruit and stir until combined. Refrigerate until ready to serve. Right before serving, garnish the salad with star fruit.

Jafar's Jewel Salad

Serves 4

Sparkling gems aren't just a part of Jafar's regal attire—he also uses them as tools to achieve his ultimate goal of becoming sultan. This bright salad features jewel-toned vegetables, making it an enticing and colourful dish.

Ingredients

1½ cups cooked bulgur, cooled

½ small yellow capsicum, chopped

3 Tbsp chopped red onion

2 Lebanese cucumbers, chopped

1 cup cherry tomatoes, halved

2 Tbsp chopped parsley

2 Tbsp lemon juice

¼ cup olive oil

¾ tsp kosher salt

¼ tsp black pepper

Directions

1. In a large bowl, combine the bulgur, capsicum, red onion, cucumbers, tomatoes and parsley.
2. In another small bowl, whisk together the lemon juice, olive oil, salt and pepper. Pour the dressing over the salad and toss to coat. Refrigerate until ready to serve.

Tip

Bulgur has a slightly nutty flavour and pleasantly chewy texture similar to brown rice. It is found in lots of dishes traditionally prepared in the Middle East.

Snacks

Makes 18

Ingredients

2 tsp olive oil

1 small leek, white and pale-green parts only, finely chopped

½ cup Solanto tomatoes, chopped

2 tsp chopped fresh basil

¼ tsp kosher salt

¼ tsp black pepper

1 refrigerated piecrust from a 425 g package

60 g goat cheese

1 egg

Tip

A pastry tamper can make the job of shaping dough for tarts much easier. (If you don't own a pastry tamper, you can use a teaspoon or even your fingers to mold/tamp down the pastry.)

Queen of Hearts Tomato Tarts

Wonderland is known for its extravagant tea parties—and its size-changing foods! The Queen of Hearts would surely love this small tart that features a heart shape and her favourite colour, red.

Directions

1. Ask an adult for help with the oven. Heat the oven to 200°C. In a small skillet over medium heat, warm the olive oil. Add the leek and cook until tender, about 5 minutes. Place in a small bowl and combine with the tomatoes, basil, salt and pepper. Set aside.
2. Use a 6.5 cm round cookie cutter to shape 18 circles from the piecrust dough, then shape 18 hearts from the remaining scraps with a mini heart cutter. When needed, gather and reroll the dough to 6 mm thickness as you work.
3. Use a pastry tamper to mold each dough round in a well of a mini cupcake pan. Evenly divide the goat cheese among the tarts, followed by the tomato mixture. Top each tart with a dough heart.
4. In a small bowl, whisk the egg with 1 tablespoon water. Brush the tarts with the egg wash, then bake until light golden brown, about 12 minutes. Serve warm.

Towering Parfait

Makes 2

Ingredients

Lemon or vanilla pudding

Fresh blueberries or blackberries

Whipped cream

If there's one place Mother Gothel knows best, it's the tall tower she lives in! This tasty snack, featuring towering layers of pudding, fruit and whipped cream, is a delicious take on her memorable home.

Directions

1. Spoon a little pudding into the bottoms of two parfait glasses. Top the pudding with a layer of fresh berries, followed by a big dollop of whipped cream.
2. Repeat step 1.
3. Add one more layer of pudding.
4. Top each parfait with a small dollop of whipped cream and garnish, if you like, with 1 or 2 fresh berries.

Tip

For another yummy version of this snack, make it with lemon yoghurt in place of the pudding.

Makes 12

Ingredients

6 large eggs

2 Tbsp mayonnaise

½ ripe avocado, diced

Kosher salt

Black pepper

3 mini kosher dill pickles

Tip

Steaming the eggs rather than boiling them makes peeling the shells a snap! If you need more guidance on how to peel eggs, ***check out page 133***.

Croco-Devilled Eggs

Captain Hook would never willingly approach a crocodile—but he just might enjoy these most *egg*-cellent stuffed eggs. Avocado gives them their green hue, while tiny slices of pickle provide their reptilian appearance.

Directions

1. Fill a large pot with 2.5 cm of water and fit a steaming basket inside. Ask an adult for help at the stove. Bring the water to a boil over medium-high heat.
2. Ask an adult to carefully place the eggs in the steaming basket. Steam 14 minutes. Just before the eggs are done, prepare an ice bath. Ask an adult to transfer the eggs to the ice bath. Cool 10 minutes.
3. Tap and gently roll each egg on your work surface to make cracks. Peel off the shells, then, with an adult's help, halve the eggs lengthwise.
4. Drop the yolk from each egg half into a small bowl. Arrange the empty egg whites on a plate. Add the mayonnaise, avocado and ¼ tsp each salt and pepper to the bowl with the yolks, and use a fork to mash and blend the mixture until smooth. Taste and adjust seasoning if you like, adding more mayonnaise for a creamier texture or salt and pepper for more flavour. Add a spoonful of filling to each egg white.
5. Trim the pickles into claws, as shown, and press them in place on the eggs.

Octo-Arm Breadsticks

Fashioned after Ursula's tentacle-like arms, these snaky breadsticks are embellished with black olive suction cups and sprinkled with cheese.

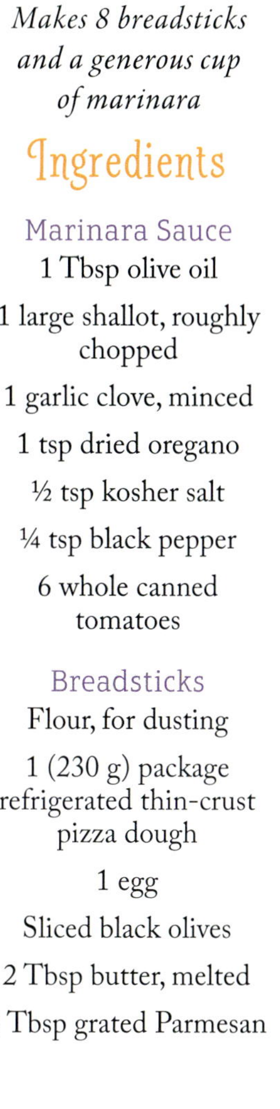

Makes 8 breadsticks and a generous cup of marinara

Ingredients

Marinara Sauce

1 Tbsp olive oil

1 large shallot, roughly chopped

1 garlic clove, minced

1 tsp dried oregano

½ tsp kosher salt

¼ tsp black pepper

6 whole canned tomatoes

Breadsticks

Flour, for dusting

1 (230 g) package refrigerated thin-crust pizza dough

1 egg

Sliced black olives

2 Tbsp butter, melted

2 Tbsp grated Parmesan

Directions

1. First make the sauce. Ask an adult for help at the stove. Warm the oil in a small skillet over medium heat. Add the shallot and cook until softened, about 2 minutes. Stir in the garlic, oregano, salt and pepper and cook 1 minute. Add the tomatoes, breaking them into small pieces with your hands. Reduce the heat to low and simmer for 10 minutes to let the flavours meld. Ask an adult for help with the immersion blender. Transfer the mixture to a bowl, then use the blender to partially puree into a chunky sauce. Cover and set aside.
2. Ask an adult for help with the oven. Heat the oven to 200°C. Line two baking trays with baking paper. Unroll the dough on a lightly floured cutting board. Use a pizza cutter to evenly slice the dough into 8 strips. Roll each strip into a long, 1.5 cm-thick rope. Place 4 ropes on each sheet, spacing them 5 cm apart. Shape them into coily tentacles, as shown.
3. In a small bowl, whisk the egg with 1 tablespoon water. Brush each breadstick with the egg wash, then flatten each one slightly and press olive slices into each, as shown. Bake until light golden, about 10 minutes. Brush the breadsticks with butter and sprinkle with Parmesan. Serve immediately with the marinara on the side for dipping.

Tip

These breadsticks are best served warm, right out of the oven.

Makes 18

Ingredients

16 whole pitted dates

¼ cup raisins

¼ cup toasted unsalted sunflower seeds

½ cup roasted and salted cashews

2 Tbsp unsweetened finely shredded coconut

¼ cup dark chocolate chips

1 tsp vegetable oil

Tip

If preferred, you can use milk chocolate chips in place of the dark chocolate for drizzling.

Striped Tiger Bites

All the animals in the jungle recognise the fearsome Shere Khan's distinctive stripes. Satisfy a growling belly with these fruit, nut and seed squares 'striped' with drizzles of chocolate.

Directions

1. Line a loaf pan with baking paper, using enough to cover the edges of the pan. With an adult's help, combine the dates, raisins, sunflower seeds, cashews and coconut in the bowl of a food processor. Pulse the mixture until it holds together but still has some small, uniform bits.
2. Spoon the mixture into the prepared loaf pan. Use another small sheet of baking paper to press the mixture so that it forms an even layer. Refrigerate for 1 hour.
3. Grab the edges of the baking paper to lift the bar from the pan and place it on a cutting board. Working on the baking paper and with an adult's help, use a sharp knife to cut the bar crosswise into 6 even strips. Slice each strip into 3 even squares.
4. In a microwave-safe bowl, combine the chocolate chips and vegetable oil. Microwave on half power for 1 minute, then stir (be careful, the bowl and its contents will be very hot) to encourage melting. If needed, return the chocolate to the microwave and heat in 10-second bursts until melted, stirring vigorously between each heating. Let the chocolate cool slightly, then place in a resealable bag and snip a corner.
5. Drizzle the melted chocolate onto the squares by gently squeezing it from the bag. Let the chocolate set before serving or packaging. Keep refrigerated until ready to eat.

Iago's Crunchy Seed Clusters

Iago has had his fill of crackers, but we bet he'd peck at these oven-toasted clusters with almonds, pepitas and a mix of flavourful seeds. Maple syrup, vanilla and shredded coconut add a touch of sweetness.

Serves 8

Ingredients

¼ cup maple syrup

1¼ tsp vanilla extract

1 egg white

¾ tsp kosher salt

½ cup raw sunflower seeds

2 Tbsp sesame seeds

2 Tbsp flax seeds

⅓ cup raw pepitas

1 cup raw almonds

¼ cup pine nuts

⅔ cup unsweetened shredded coconut

2 Tbsp unrefined coconut oil, melted

Directions

1. Ask an adult for help with the oven. Heat the oven to 160°C and line a baking tray with baking paper. In a small bowl, stir together the maple syrup, vanilla, egg white and salt. Set aside. In a large bowl, combine all the remaining ingredients. Stir to evenly coat the mixture with the oil. Add the egg mixture and stir to coat.
2. Spread the mixture on the prepared baking sheet in an even layer. Bake for 20 minutes, then have an adult use a spatula to flip the mixture (it's okay if it breaks into smaller pieces). Bake for 8 minutes more. Let cool completely on the pan (it will crisp up as it cools) before breaking into bite-size pieces.

Tip

For the best results, be sure not to overbake the clusters or they may turn bitter. The ingredients should look toasty but not dark brown.

Beverages

Serves 4

Ingredients

4 cups of your favourite prepared lemonade (a light-coloured drink works best), chilled

Blue food colouring

Lemon slices, for garnish

Special Equipment

Star-shaped ice or food mould

Night Howler Lemonade

Deputy Mayor Dawn Bellwether uses the strange Night Howler flower to make trouble in Zootopia! Inspired by the flower's bright colour, this blue lemonade is a more dramatic take on a classic summer drink.

Directions

1. Fill the mould with water and freeze until solid, about 3 hours.
2. In a large jug, stir together the lemonade with 2 drops food colouring. If needed, add another drop or two to reach the desired hue.
3. Evenly divide the drink into glasses and add a few star ice cubes. Garnish with lemon slices and serve.

Blueberry Sparkler

Just like Dr. Facilier, you can easily make your own homemade potion—a bubbly violet-coloured soft drink that is refreshing and fun to drink.

Serves about 16

Ingredients

1 lemon

3 cups blueberries, plus more for garnish

1 (2.5 cm) piece fresh ginger, sliced

1½ cups sugar

Ice

Sparkling or mineral water

Lemon slices for garnish (optional)

Directions

1. Use a vegetable peeler to remove half the rind from the lemon. Ask an adult for help at the stove. Place the rind in a large saucepan, along with the blueberries, ginger, sugar and 2 cups of water (regular, not sparkling). Bring to a boil, then reduce the heat to low and simmer for 20 minutes. Let cool completely.
2. Strain the syrup into a clean jar. To make each sparkler, fill an small glass with ice. Add 2 tablespoons syrup, then top it off with sparkling or mineral water. If you'd like, garnish with fresh blueberries and a lemon slice. Serve immediately.

Tip

The outermost part of a citrus rind (also called zest) can be used to add lots of flavour to a recipe. Here it's used to make the syrup taste lemony. Don't know how to remove zest? ***Check out the Glossary on page 141 for instructions.***

Makes 2

Ingredients

Green liquid food colouring (optional)

350 ml green or clear lemon and lime soft drink

4 scoops lemon or lime sorbet

Sour lollies or jubes for garnish

2 bamboo skewers

Tip

A slice of fruit would make a fun garnish for this float too.

Sour Bill's Citrus Float

Scoops of fruit sorbet and fizzy lemon and lime soft drink make this foamy concoction both sweet and sour—just like Sour Bill. To feel like you're inside the game of *Sugar Rush*, you can garnish each glass with gumdrops and sour candies.

Directions

1. In a tall glass, stir together a drop of food colouring, if using, with a splash of soft drink. Add 2 scoops of sorbet, then top it off with half of the remaining soft drink. Repeat with a second glass.
2. Ask an adult for help with threading a few lollies onto each skewer (be careful of the sharp point). Slide a skewer into each glass. Enjoy immediately.

Savanna Sunset Slushie

Even Scar's dark plot to become king can't cast a shadow over the glowing Pride Lands sunset. This icy pink-and-gold slushie captures its colourful beauty and makes a refreshing treat on a warm summer day.

Makes 2

Ingredients

¼ cup frozen orange juice

4 cups ice

¼ cup frozen pink cordial (raspberry or strawberry)

2 maraschino cherries with stems, for garnish

Directions

1. Ask an adult for help with the blender. In the blender, combine the orange juice with 2 cups of ice and 6 tablespoons of water. Blend into a slush, then divide evenly between two glasses.
2. Rinse the blender's jug with cool water, then add the pink cordial concentrate, remaining 2 cups ice, and 6 tablespoons water. Puree into slush. Add half the mixture to each glass. Use a straw to gently blend the edges of the slushie layers in each glass, as shown. Top each with a cherry. Serve immediately.

Tip

Make this drink extra special by serving it in a fancy glass. Just make sure it has see-through sides!

Serves 4

Ingredients

4 cups apple cider

2 cinnamon sticks, plus more for garnish

6 orange slices, plus more for garnish

4 star anise pods

4 whole cloves

1 Tbsp honey (optional)

Tip

Serve the cider with your favourite pastry.

Witch's Brew

The Queen is known for brewing a mixture that casts a sleepy spell. But a mug of this steamy drink—made with apple cider, oranges and spices—is simply warm and cosy! Letting the mixture steep for several minutes after the cider simmers will add more flavour.

Directions

1. Ask an adult for help at the stove. In a medium saucepan, combine the cider, cinnamon sticks, orange slices, star anise and cloves. Warm over medium heat until the mixture begins to bubble around the edges. Reduce the heat to low and simmer 20 minutes. Turn off the heat and let sit 5 minutes more. Stir in the honey, if using.
2. Set a mesh strainer over a bowl. With an adult's help, pour the cider through the strainer and discard the solids. Pour the cider into mugs and garnish each with a cinnamon stick and orange slice. Serve warm.

Chocolate Mud Puddle

The last thing Gaston wants to do is soil his beautiful appearance! But sometimes his actions land him in muddy waters. This cup of hot chocolate topped with mini marshmallows offers an edible homage with its own surprise twist: chocolate hazelnut spread.

Directions

1. In a medium saucepan, whisk together the drinking chocolate powder and ½ cup milk until the chocolate is dissolved. Ask an adult for help at the stove. Stir in the remaining 1½ cups milk and the hazelnut spread, then set over medium heat. Warm until the mixture is hot and the hazelnut spread has dissolved, about 3 minutes.
2. With an adult's help, pour the hot chocolate into mugs. Garnish each with marshmallows and a sprinkle of drinking chocolate powder. Serve immediately.

Serves 2

Ingredients

1 Tbsp drinking chocolate powder, plus more for garnish

2 cups milk of your choice

3 Tbsp chocolate hazelnut spread

Marshmallows, for garnish

Tip

Pack this cocoa in a thermos and bring it along on a hike for a warming treat. It can easily be doubled, so there's plenty to share.

Sweets

Makes 8

Ingredients

8 round chocolate biscuits

30 g dark or semisweet chocolate, chopped

2 tsp vegetable oil

8 large marshmallows

2 strips red sour straps

8 purple jelly beans

¼ cup white frosting

Special Equipment

Toothpicks

Tip

To help the chocolate set quicker, place the hats in the refrigerator for 10 minutes at the end of step 3.

Chocolate Top Hats

Dr. Facilier is rarely seen without his signature top hat! This treat, styled as the villain's infamous chapeau, conceals a sweet secret—a puffy marshmallow under an irresistible layer of chocolate.

Directions

1. Arrange the cookies on a baking tray in a single layer. Fill a saucepan with 15 ml of water and set a heat-safe bowl over the top, making sure the bottom of the bowl does not touch the water. Add the chocolate to the bowl.
2. Ask an adult for help at the stove. Heat the saucepan with the bowl on medium heat. Melt the chocolate, stirring frequently so that it heats evenly. Once melted, remove from the heat and stir in the vegetable oil.
3. Stand a marshmallow on the end of a fork. Working over the bowl with the melted chocolate, spoon the chocolate over the marshmallow to cover the top and sides. Gently tap the fork on the side of the bowl to remove the excess chocolate, then use a toothpick to slide the marshmallow onto one of the biscuits. Repeat with the remaining marshmallows, chocolate and biscuits. Let the chocolate set.
4. Trim the tape candy into 8 strips. Use the frosting to attach a strip and purple jelly bean 'feather' to each hat, as shown.

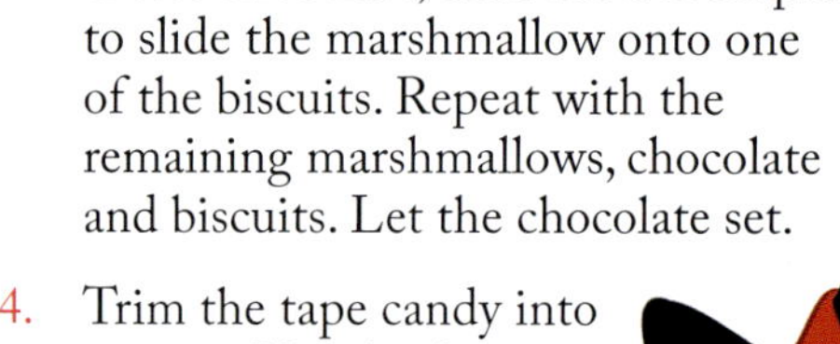

Flame Meringue Pops

When Hades is in a good mood, the flames atop his head are a cool blue—but make him angry, and they'll quickly roar to orange and red! These pops were designed with Hades's calmer state in mind, but should the feeling strike, you can replace the blue with a fierier colour.

Makes 6 to 8

Ingredients

2 egg whites

⅛ tsp cream of tartar

¼ tsp vanilla extract

Pinch kosher salt

½ cup sugar

Blue food colouring (or other colour of choice)

15 cm lollipop sticks

Directions

1. Ask an adult for help with the oven. Heat the oven to 100°C and line two baking trays with baking paper. In a stand mixer fitted with a whisk attachment and set on medium speed, whip the egg whites with the cream of tartar, vanilla and salt until frothy. Add a tablespoon sugar, increase the mixer's speed to medium high, and continue to whip until the sugar is dissolved. Keep adding the sugar 1 tablespoon at a time, letting the sugar dissolve between each addition, until stiff peaks form and all the sugar has been added, about 12 minutes.
2. Add a few drops of food colouring to the meringue and gently stir a few times to swirl, but do not fully blend the colour. Transfer the mixture to a piping bag fitted with a large star tip.
3. Lay a lollipop stick 8 cm from the edge of one of the prepared pans. Hold the stick in place and pipe the meringue in a flame pattern, as shown, covering the top 5 cm of the stick. Repeat with the remaining sticks and meringue mixture.
4. Bake the pops for 2 hours, then turn off the heat and let them cool completely in the oven, about 2 hours more. To prevent cracking, do not open the oven door as they cook or cool.

Tip

Check out page 134 *for a visual guide to creating these pops—and* ***page 140*** *for more information about piping bags!*

Makes 12

Ingredients

1¼ cups white frosting

Red food colouring

4 chocolate chew lollies

12 plain cupcakes

12 large white gumdrops

12 small white gumdrops

24 white sugared almonds

24 white pearl sprinkles

12 jumbo star sprinkles

Tip

Experiment with different colours, shapes and sizes of lollies to create a castle of your own design.

Sugar Rush Castle Cupcakes

King Candy's home-sweet-home comes to life with this fanciful cupcake. Pearl sprinkles and sugar-coated gumdrops give this edible castle some extra sparkle.

Directions

1. Tint 1 cup of the frosting pink with the red food colouring. Use your fingers to flatten each chocolate chew lolly and trim 3 small doors from each, as shown.

2. Working with one cupcake at a time, cover the top with pink frosting. Press on a large white gumdrop, then use some of the remaining white frosting to attach a small white gumdrop on top. Stand a sugared almond on each side of the white gumdrop, as shown, then use frosting to top each almond with a white pearl sprinkle. Finish the castle with a chocolate door
and star sprinkle top (attached with frosting). Repeat with the remaining cupcakes and ingredients.

Black Cat Doughnuts

Lady Tremaine's loyal pet, Lucifer, is purr-fectly captured in this plain doughnut turned decorated dessert, right down to his mischievous grin. It's best served with a glass of milk, of course!

Makes 2

Ingredients

Green food writer

Black food writer

4 yellow sugared almonds

½ cup chocolate frosting

3 Tbsp white frosting

2 plain cake doughnuts

2 pink jelly beans

4 chocolate-covered almonds

Directions

1. Use the food writers to draw an eye and pupil in the centre of each sugared almond, as shown. Place 3 tablespoons of the chocolate frosting and all the white frosting in separate piping bags, each fitted with a small writing tip. Place the remaining chocolate frosting in a piping bag fitted with a mini star tip.
2. Using the chocolate frosting in the bag with the star tip, cover the top half of each doughnut with tiny dots of frosting, as shown. Press a pair of almond eyes and a pink jelly bean nose onto each. Trim the rounded chocolate end from each almond, and attach them with chocolate frosting, as shown. Use the white frosting to pipe a centre in each ear.
3. Using the chocolate frosting in the bag with the writing tip, draw a mouth on each doughnut, as shown. Finish by piping on white frosting whiskers.

Tip

A food writer is a marker that is filled with edible ink. You can find them online or at craft or cooking stores that sell baking supplies.

Makes 18

Ingredients

3 Tbsp granulated sugar, plus more for rolling

½ tsp ground cinnamon

1 sheet puff pastry dough (from a 500 g package)

3 Tbsp butter, melted

1 Tbsp coarse sugar

Special Equipment

Toothpicks

Tip

Turn to page 135 *for step-by-step instructions on how to shape these special treats.*

Elephant Ears

The hyenas Shenzi, Banzai and Ed serve as loyal minions to the nefarious Scar, aiding in his plot to rule over the animal kingdom. The trio can often be found in the Elephant Graveyard on the edges of the Pride Lands—but this delicious dessert is a lighter homage to their shadowy stomping grounds.

Directions

1. Ask an adult for help with the oven. Heat the oven to 200°C and line two baking trays with baking paper. In a small bowl, stir together the sugar and cinnamon.
2. Sprinkle your work surface with sugar. Using a rolling pin or similar tool, roll the dough out into a 30 cm square. Brush it generously with butter and sprinkle with the cinnamon sugar. Roll once more to press the sugar into the dough. Use a toothpick to make a small mark in the centre of the square. Starting at one end, roll the dough up into a tube, stopping at the centre mark. Repeat with the opposite side of the dough to form a tube with two curled sides.
3. With an adult's help, cut the tube crosswise into 2 cm slices. Arrange on the baking sheets, spreading them 5 cm apart. Brush them with the remaining butter and sprinkle with coarse sugar. Bake until crisp and puffed, about 10 minutes. Let them cool before serving.

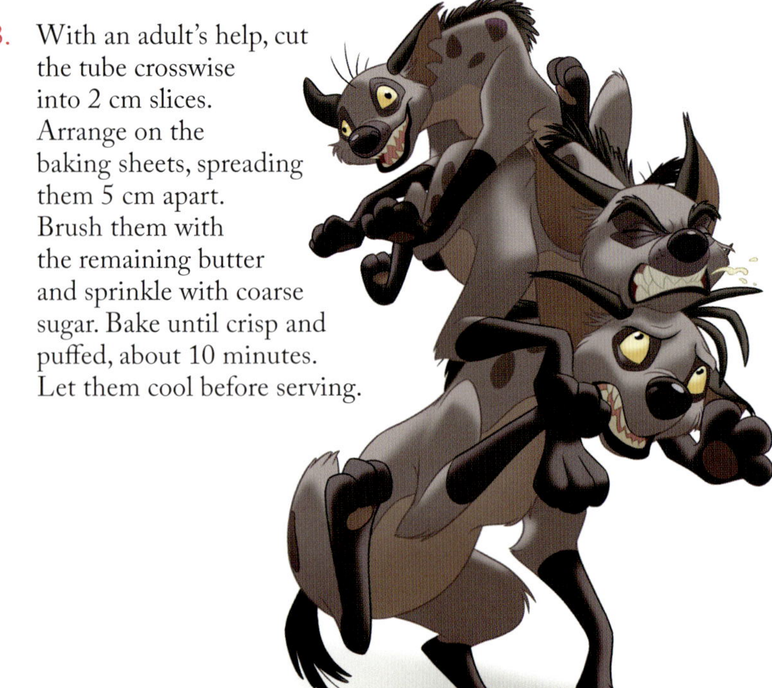

Treasure Trove Coconut Ice Cream

Serves 8

Ingredients

½ cup shredded sweetened coconut

1 (400 ml) can sweetened condensed milk

3 Tbsp cream of coconut

1¾ cups heavy cream

½ cup chocolate chunks, roughly chopped

This rich and creamy no-churn ice cream is filled with delicious treasures, including chocolate chunks and toasted coconut. Be sure to use cream of coconut, a sugary flavoured syrup used in drinks and desserts, rather than coconut cream for flavouring.

Directions

1. Ask an adult for help with the oven. Heat the oven to 180°C. Spread the shredded coconut on a baking tray. Toast it until it's lightly golden, about 8 to 10 minutes. Transfer it immediately to a plate and let it cool completely.
2. In a large bowl, whisk together the sweetened condensed milk and cream of coconut. In another bowl, use a hand mixer set on medium speed to whip the heavy cream until stiff peaks form, about 2 minutes. Gently fold the whipped cream into the milk mixture, being careful not to deflate it by mixing too long.
3. Set aside 2 tablespoons of the chocolate chunks. Fold the remaining chocolate into the cream, then fold in the coconut. Pour the mixture into a loaf pan. Gently smooth the top with the back of a spoon, then sprinkle with the reserved chocolate.
4. Cover the ice cream with plastic wrap, then freeze until solid, about 6 hours.

Tip

No ice cream machine? No problem! The only equipment you'll need to make this dessert is a hand mixer.

Makes 12

Ingredients

1 (450 g) package refrigerated sugar cookie dough

6 Tbsp flour

2 cups icing sugar, sifted

4 tsp meringue powder

1 Tbsp glucose syrup

Edible silver dust

Gold sprinkles

Tip

If you've made other desserts in this book, you may already be familiar with a piping bag! But if not, ***check out page 140*** *for more info.*

Magic Mirror Sugar Cookies

You won't see your reflection in these cookies, but their silver and gold embellishments are nearly as enchanting as the Magic Mirror that speaks to the Queen. You'll need some time and patience to make a batch, but the end result will be nothing short of bewitching.

Directions

1. Ask an adult for help with the oven. Heat the oven to 180°C and line two baking trays with baking paper. In a large bowl, break the dough into several pieces, then toss with the flour. Use your hands to knead the flour into the dough.
2. On a lightly floured surface, roll the dough out to 5 mm thickness. Use a 6-to-8 cm oval cookie cutter to shape the dough. Arrange the cookies on a prepared baking tray, spacing them 5 cm apart. Gather and reroll the dough as needed. Freeze the unbaked cookies for 10 minutes.
3. Bake the cookies until lightly golden on the bottom, about 12 minutes. Let cool on the pan for 5 minutes, then transfer to a rack to cool completely.
4. Once the cookies have cooled, use a hand mixer to blend together the icing sugar, meringue powder and glucose syrup with ¼ cup water until thickened. If the icing is too stiff, add 1 more teaspoon of water and stir once again (up to 3 teaspoons can be added if needed). Transfer the mixture to a piping bag fitted with a writing tip.
5. Use the icing to pipe an oval in the centre of each cookie, leaving a 1.5 cm border. Let dry, then brush with silver dust. Use the remaining icing to attach gold sprinkles around the edge of each cookie. Let the icing set several hours before serving.

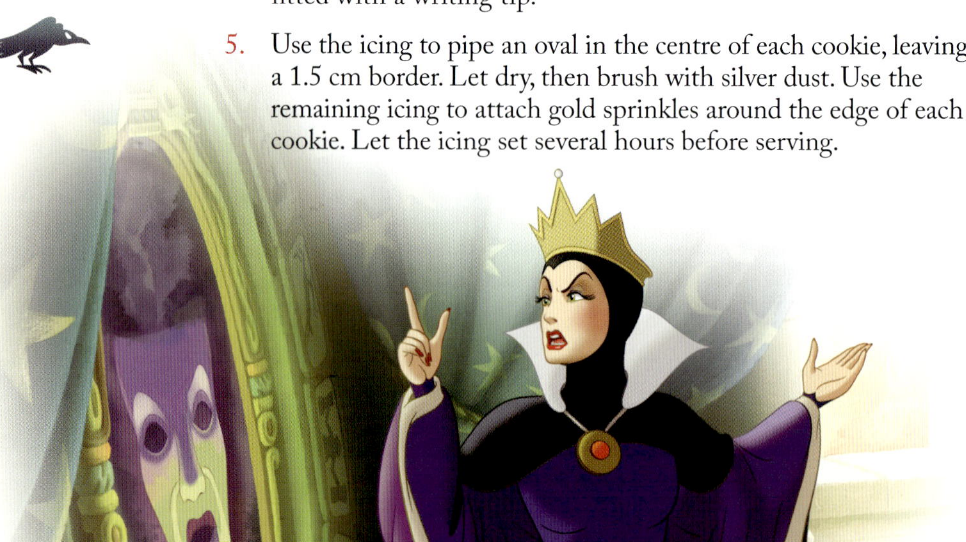

Captain Hook Brownie Bites

Reel in your crew with a chocolaty delight that recalls one of Captain Hook's most memorable features.

Makes 12

Ingredients

⅓ cup white candy melts

6 black candy melts

1½ cups white frosting

Red gel food colouring

12 store-bought brownie bites

Directions

1. Line a baking tray with baking paper. Combine the candy melts in a small microwave-safe bowl, and melt according to the package directions. Transfer the candy to a piping bag fitted with a small writing tip, then pipe 12 hook shapes onto the prepared pan. Let the candy set.
2. Meanwhile, place ½ cup frosting in a small bowl and add in the red food colouring. Transfer it to a piping bag fitted with a large round tip. Place the remaining frosting in a piping bag fitted with a large star tip.
3. Pipe a large dollop of red frosting onto the top of each brownie bite by centreing the piping tip atop the brownie, holding it 5 mm from the surface and pushing the frosting out so that it spreads to form a circle, as shown. Repeat the technique to add a dollop of white frosting to each brownie. Finish by adding a candy hook to each. Keep cool until ready to serve.

Tip

If you like, you can replace the brownie bites in this recipe with mini chocolate cupcakes.

Makes 12

Ingredients

⅓ cup dark chocolate chips

⅓ cup green candy melts

24 plain chocolate cookies

12 jumbo heart sprinkles

½ cup your favourite chocolate frosting

Tip

To let something 'set' means to let it harden! Be patient when the chocolate is cooling to ensure you're getting the special shapes for this cookie just right.

Maleficent's Triple Chocolate Sandwich Cookies

Mesmerise chocolate lovers with a spellbinding sweet that looks just like Maleficent! These cookies come together like magic and feature chocolate both inside and out.

Directions

1. Line a baking tray with baking paper. Melt the chocolate chips according to the package directions and transfer to a piping bag fitted with a small writing tip. Pipe 12 sets of horns, as shown, onto the baking paper. Let the chocolate set.
2. Meanwhile, in a small, heat-safe bowl, melt the green candy melts according to the package directions. Place the melted candy in a piping bag fitted with a small writing tip and use it to create the outline of Maleficent's face on 12 of the cookies. Let set for 3 minutes. Working with one cookie at a time, use the melted candy to fill in the centre of the face and quickly place a heart sprinkle near the bottom, as shown. Repeat with the remaining candy and sprinkles. Let set completely.
3. Spread 2 teaspoons frosting onto each of the remaining cookies. Press a set of chocolate horns into the frosting at the top edge of the cookie, then sandwich with a cookie face.

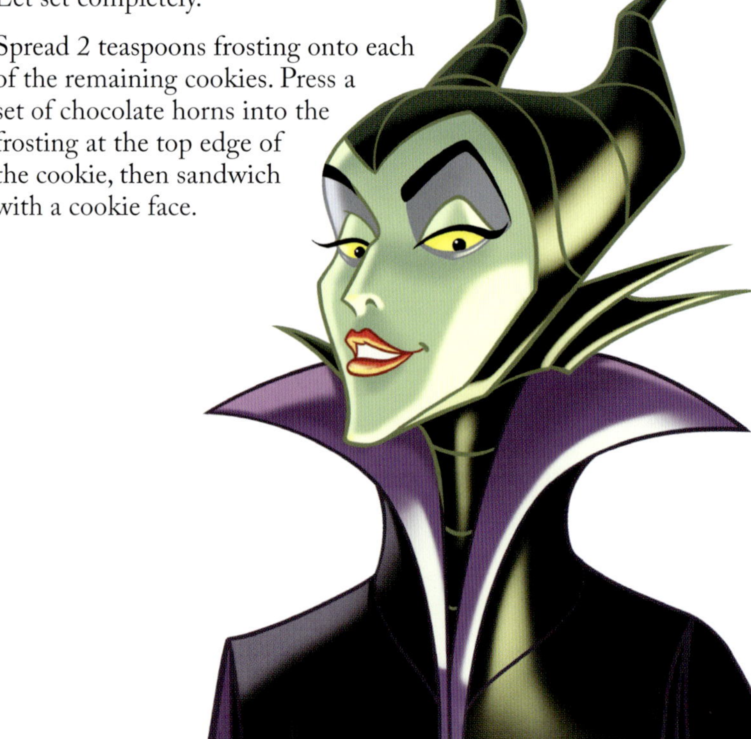

Cruella Cookies

The sleek black-and-white colouring on these sugar cookies comes from dipping them in chocolate—a decadent tribute to the very fashionable Cruella.

Makes about 36

Ingredients

1 batch sugar cookie dough (store-bought or using your favourite recipe)

1 cup white chocolate chips

1 cup dark chocolate chips

Jumbo heart sprinkles

Directions

1. Ask an adult for help with the oven. Heat the oven to 180°C and line two baking trays with baking paper. Roll out the cookie dough to 5 mm thickness. Use a 6-to-8 cm round cutter to shape the dough into circles. Arrange them on the baking trays, spacing them 5 cm apart. Gather and reroll the dough as needed.
2. Bake the cookies until set and slightly crisp, about 12 minutes, turning them once halfway through. Let the cookies cool on the trays for 5 minutes, then transfer them to a rack to cool completely. Cover the baking trays with fresh paper and set aside.
3. Melt the white chocolate chips in a heat-safe bowl according to the package directions. Dip the edge of each cookie into the white chocolate, as shown, letting the excess fall back into the bowl. If needed, use the flat edge of a butter knife to scrape away any extra chocolate from the backs of the cookies. Place the cookies on a prepared baking tray and let the chocolate set. Repeat the steps with the dark chocolate, dipping the opposite side. Attach a heart sprinkle mouth to each cookie with a bit of melted chocolate applied with a toothpick. Let set completely before serving.

Makes 4

Ingredients

8 large strawberries

Whipped cream

Tip

Turn to page 136 *for step-by-step instructions on how to create the rose shape. Don't worry if it's not perfect—the result will still be delicious!*

Edible Roses

The Queen of Hearts prefers that the roses in her garden are always red. Fortunately, these edible strawberry roses are red too—with a dash of white whipped cream for delicious flavour.

Directions

1. Wash the strawberries in cold water and pat them dry with a paper towel.
2. Ask an adult to help you with the knife. Then slice off the strawberries' leafy tops.
3. Stand one of the berries flat side (stem side) down. Create an outer row of 4 rose petals around the tip by slicing three-quarters of the way down through the berry on all 4 sides.
4. To finish the rose, cut a second strawberry in half from top to bottom. Then cut one of the halves into several slices. Tuck 3 or 4 of the slices between the tip and outer petals of the first berry.
5. Repeat with the remaining strawberries. Store any leftover strawberry pieces in the refrigerator to enjoy as a snack later.
6. Put a spoonful of whipped cream onto a plate. Set a strawberry rose on top, then repeat with remaining berries and whipped cream and serve.

Step-by-Step Instructions

Villains know that crafting the perfect potions and brews takes practice! Turn the page for step-by-step photos for some of the recipes—and you'll be a pro at creating dishes that are both delicious and eye-catching in no time.

Baguette Breakfast Beaks

Prep your baguette for a tasty baked-egg filling with this step-by-step guide.

1. Have an adult use a serrated knife to trim a rectangle from the centre of the loaf, leaving a 1.3 cm border and being careful not to cut all the way through.

2. Pull away the rectangle of bread and discard or use to make croutons for another time.

See the full recipe on page 20!

Mini Tamatoa Seaweed Rolls

Roll up a satisfying veggie snack with this step-by-step guide.

1. Cover a sheet of nori with rice.

2. Add a few slices of each vegetable to the centre of the roll.

3. Bring one end of the nori up and over the vegetables, as shown.

4. Continue to roll the nori until a cone is formed.

See the full recipe on page 34!

Fishy Sticks

Cut perfectly portioned sticks without a ruler using this step-by-step guide.

1. With an adult's help, stand the tofu on a short end and use a sharp knife to halve it lengthwise.

2. Lay the tofu down and, keeping the pieces stacked, halve it once more. You should now have 4 pieces total, 2 on top and 2 on bottom of stack.

3. Slice each stacked half into 3 pieces. You should now have 12 pieces total, six on top and six on bottom of stack.

4. The final 12 pieces should now look like the photo above.

See the full recipe on page 58!

Croco-Devilled Eggs

Crack and peel a hard-boiled egg with ease using this step-by-step guide.

1. Tap the large end of a hard-boiled egg on your work surface to crack it.

2. Lay the egg on its side and make several more cracks. Turn it a few times to make cracks all the way around the shell.

3. Use your fingers to roll the egg back and forth to make even more cracks.

4. Starting at the large end of the egg, peel away the shell, making sure to get underneath the membrane between the shell and egg. It should come off in large strips.

See the full recipe on page 82!

Flame Meringue Pops

Pipe the perfect pop with this step-by-step guide.

1. Use one hand to hold a lollipop stick in place. Use the other hand to pipe the meringue onto the stick, starting 5 cm from the top.

2. Continue to pipe the meringue, making sure each strip is connected. For more dimension layer a few dollops of meringue on top of the other strips.

See the full recipe on page 108!

Elephant Ears

Roll and slice a batch of irresistible cinnamon-sugar pastries with this step-by-step guide.

1. Roll the dough out into a 30.5 cm square and cover it in butter and cinnamon sugar.
2. Use a toothpick to mark the centre of the square.
3. Starting at one end, roll the dough to the centre of the square up to the hatch mark.

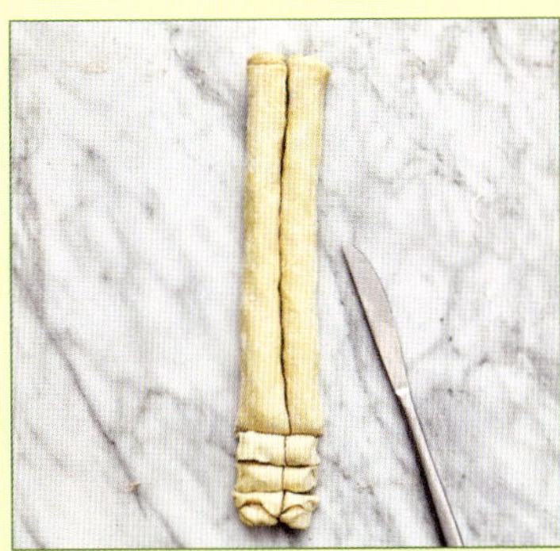

4. Repeat with the other side.
5. Cut the tube crosswise into 1.3 cm-thick slices.

Go to page 114 for the full recipe!

Edible Roses

Create edible blooms with this step-by-step guide.

1. With an adult's help, use a paring knife to trim the top from a strawberry.

2. Make 4 slits around the base of the berry, taking care not to cut all the way through. Set the berry aside.

3. Trim a second berry into very thin slices.

4. Layer the berry slices in the slits of the prepared berry to create petals.

Go to page 126 for the full recipe!

Dietary Considerations

Food allergies or preferences? No problem! Use this guide to check which recipes accommodate dairy-free, gluten-free, vegan and vegetarian diets—and which can be adapted to let everyone enjoy the meal. Recipes not included below may not be suitable for special diets. If using store-bought ingredients, always check the label or packaging to make sure they meet your dietary needs.

DF = Dairy-Free (no milk products, but can include eggs) / GF = Gluten-Free / V = Vegan / VEG = Vegetarian

Breakfast

The Queen's Bewitching Apple Bowl DF / GF / V / VEG
Spotted Scones VEG
Rosy Red Porridge DF / V / VEG
Dozen-Egg Frittata GF / VEG
Blackberry French Toast Casserole VEG

Lunch

Kronk's Spinach Puffs VEG
Smoky Chicken Salad Cups DF / GF / V or VEG (if chicken and mayo are substituted with vegan alternatives)
Mini Tamatoa Seaweed Rolls DF / GF / V / VEG
Roaring Pizza Pockets VEG (if pepperoni is substituted with a vegetarian alternative)
Playing-Card Sandwiches DF / GF (if made with gluten-free bread) / V / VEG
Golden Squash and Apple Soup GF / V (if chicken broth and butter are substituted with vegan equivalents) / VEG (if made with vegetable broth)
Lady Tremaine's Emerald Grain Bowl DF / GF / V (if honey is replaced with maple syrup) / VEG

Dinner

Captain Hook's Stuffed Shells VEG
Spiced Chicken Kebabs GF
Shape-Shifting Pesto Pasta DF (if regular Parmesan is substituted with a vegan alternative) / GF (if made with gluten-free pasta) / VEG (if sausage is substituted with veggie alternative)
Kaa's Aloo Gobi DF / GF / V / VEG
Gaston's Chicken Drumsticks DF / GF
Fishy Sticks DF / GF (if made with gluten-free panko and gluten-free flour) / V / VEG
Dr. Facilier's Baking Tray Prawn Boil DF / GF
Serpent Stew DF

Sides

Yzma's Roasted Broccoli with Parmesan GF / V (if regular Parmesan is substituted with a vegan alternative) / VEG
Maleficent's Purple Potato Salad DF / GF / V (if mayo is substituted with a vegan alternative) / VEG
Black and White Bean Salad DF / GF / V / VEG
Ursula's Sea Bubble Berry Salad DF / GF / V (if honey is replaced with maple syrup) / VEG
Jafar's Jewel Salad DF / V / VEG

Snacks

Queen of Hearts Tomato Tarts VEG
Towering Parfait GF / VEG
Croco-Devilled Eggs DF / GF / VEG
Octo-Arm Breadsticks VEG
Striped Tiger Bites GF / V (if made with vegan chocolate) / VEG
Iago's Crunchy Seed Clusters DF / GF / VEG

Beverages

Night Howler Lemonade DF / GF / V / VEG
Blueberry Sparkler DF / GF / V / VEG
Sour Bill's Citrus Float DF / GF / V / VEG
Savanna Sunset Slushie DF / GF / V / VEG
Witch's Brew DF / GF / V (if honey is omitted or replaced with maple syrup) / VEG
Chocolate Mud Puddle DF (if made with nondairy milk) / GF / VEG (if marshmallows are substituted with vegan marshmallows)

Sweets

Chocolate Top Hats VEG (if marshmallows are substituted with a vegan alternative)
Flame Meringue Pops DF / VEG
***Sugar Rush* Castle Cupcakes** VEG
Black Cat Doughnuts VEG
Elephant Ears V (if butter and puff pastry are vegan options) / VEG
Treasure Trove Coconut Ice Cream GF / VEG
Magic Mirror Sugar Cookies VEG
Captain Hook Brownie Bites VEG
Maleficent's Triple Chocolate Sandwich Cookies VEG
Cruella Cookies VEG
Edible Roses GF / VEG

Glossary

A

Andouille sausage—a type of smoked sausage, made of pork

Apple cider vinegar—a type of vinegar made from apple juice

B

Baguette—a long, narrow loaf of French bread with a crisp crust

Bake—to cook ingredients in an oven using indirect heat around the food. Many ovens must first be set to a bake setting before the temperature is adjusted.

Baking paper—heat-resistant paper used to line a baking tray so cookies and other foods won't stick to the pan when you bake them

Baking tray—a flat metal pan used for baking, especially for sweets like cookies, biscuits or breads

Blend—to combine two or more ingredients into a smooth mixture

C

Candy melts—coloured candy chips that are melted and used for baking and decorating

Challah bread—a braided bread of Ashkenazi Jewish origin that is made with eggs, flour, sugar, yeast and water

Chives—a green, grasslike herb with a mild onion flavour. It's often used as a garnish

Chop—to cut an ingredient into pieces that are roughly the same size

Chorizo—a type of sausage made of pork

Cloves (garlic)—each segment of a garlic plant bulb

Cloves (spice)—made from the dried flower buds of a tropical tree

Coarse sugar—a large crystal sugar mainly used as a topping on baked goods

Coconut aminos—a salty, dark brown condiment made from coconut sap

Cream of tartar—a dry powder often used in baking

Creole seasoning—a blend of zesty herbs and spices often used to cook traditional New Orleans dishes

Crumbled—broken or rubbed into small pieces

Cumin—a spice made from the seeds of a herb in the parsley family

D

Dice—to cut foods into small cubes (typically 6 mm wide)

Dill—a sweet, delicate, green herb harvested from the flowering tops of dill plants

Dragon fruit—a sweet, tropical fruit with a bright magenta- or golden-coloured skin and seedy, white or bright pink flesh

Drizzle—to slowly pour a thin stream of liquid or a melted ingredient over another food

Dust—to lightly sprinkle a powdery ingredient, such as icing sugar or flour. Rolling pins are often dusted with flour to keep them from sticking to piecrust, cookie dough or other foods that are rolled out

E

Edamame—a type of soybean that is especially popular in East Asian cuisines

Extract—a concentrated flavouring made by soaking certain foods, such as vanilla beans, in water or other liquids

F

Feta—a crumbly, white cheese of Greek origin most often made of sheep or goat's milk

Fold—to gently blend ingredients by using a spatula to cut through the centre of the mixture and then flip one half over the other. Stiff-beaten egg whites are often folded, rather than stirred, into cake and soufflé recipes to keep as much air in the batter as possible

G

Garam masala—a spice blend widely used in Indian cuisines

Garnish—to decorate a prepared recipe with an herb, a fruit or another edible ingredient that adds colour and/or texture

Grate—to shred foods, such as coconut, carrots, cheese or chocolate, into bits or flakes by rubbing them against a grater

Grill— to cook ingredients using direct heat over the food. Most ovens have grill settings

Ground—when a dry ingredient has been broken up into very small pieces, often with a powderlike texture

I

Icing sugar—a finely ground form of sugar, also known as powdered sugar

K

Kitchen scissors—scissors made specifically for cutting food

Knead—to repeatedly fold and press together dough until it is smooth and stretchy. Kneading traps air bubbles produced by the yeast, which is what makes the dough rise

M

Marinate—to soak food in a flavoured liquid for an extended period of time so that the food absorbs the flavour before cooking. The flavoured liquid is called a marinade

Meringue—a type of dessert traditionally made with whipped egg whites and sugar

Mince—to chop ingredients, such as garlic cloves, gingerroot or fresh herbs, extra fine. This evenly distributes the flavour in the dish you are cooking

Mixed herbs—a blend of dried herbs

Muffuletta—a type of sandwich originated by Italian Americans in New Orleans

N

Nori—thin sheets of dried, mildly sweet seaweed, mainly used in Japanese cuisine as a food wrap for sushi

Nutmeg—a spice made from the seed of a tropical tree

O

Oregano—a herb commonly used in Mediterranean cuisines

P

Paprika—a spice made from ground dried bell or chili peppers

Parfait—a layered dessert usually featuring a soft, sweet ingredient (like whipped cream, custard or ice cream), and fruit that's served in a tall, narrow glass

Pastry tamper—a tool used to press dough into tart or pie pans so that it's even

Pat—to gently tap dough with the palm of your hand

Pepitas—a kind of pumpkin seed commonly used in Mexican cooking

Pinch—a small amount of a dry ingredient, such as salt or a ground spice, added to a recipe with your fingertips

Piping bag—a cone-shaped bag with a pointed end used to dispense batter, frosting or other soft food mixtures. To use one, snip the pointed end of the bag and fit a piping tip inside. Fill the bag with your chosen frosting or topping, then twist the open end to seal the bag. Pipe the mixture by pushing it from the sealed end

Produce—fresh fruits and/or vegetables

Puff pastry—a light, flaky pastry made by combining thin layers of butter and dough

Purée—to blend food until it is completely smooth

R

Rice vinegar—a vinegar made from fermented rice wine. Popular in China, this type of vinegar has a much sweeter taste than Western vinegars

S

Saucepan—a high-sided pan, usually with a handle, and meant for cooking foods on a stovetop

Seltzer water—water that has been combined with carbon dioxide to make it bubbly

Separate egg whites—to divide egg whites (the clear portion of the egg) from their yolks (the yellow portion). To do it, crack the egg and pour its contents into one of the shell halves. Working over a bowl, tip the yolk back and forth into each shell half, letting the white fall into the bowl. Slide the yolk into a separate bowl

Serrated knife—a small utensil used to delicately peel or cut fruits and vegetables

Shallot—a purple-skinned, bulb-shaped onion with a mild flavour

Shred—to pull or cut an ingredient into many thin strips

Simmer—to cook food on the stovetop in liquid heated just to the point at which small bubbles rise to the surface

Skillet—a flat-bottomed, shallow pan with a long handle used for cooking on a stovetop

Snip—to use kitchen scissors to cut an ingredient into small pieces

Soften—to warm an ingredient such as butter (either by setting it out at room temperature or heating it in a microwave) until it is easy to combine with a mixture

Spring onion— a long, green onion with a small bulb on its end

Star anise—a star-shaped, licorice-flavoured fruit that is dried and used as a spice. It is used in many Asian cuisines

Star fruit—a yellow, sweet, tangy tropical fruit that has a distinctive star shape

Steep—to soak an ingredient in water or another liquid to infuse the liquid with the ingredient's flavour

Strain—to remove liquid from an ingredient or mixture by pouring it into a colander, metal sieve or cheesecloth. The solids are trapped in the colander, sieve or cloth and liquid drains away

Sugared almonds—a toasted almond that is coated with a hard, coloured sugar shell

Sweetened condensed milk—milk that is blended with sugar and simmered until half or more of the water of its water has evaporated. The remaining liquid is thick and creamy

T

Toss—to mix solid ingredients by gently combining them

To taste—to add just enough of a certain ingredient, typically one or more spices, to improve the flavour of a dish

Turmeric—a brightly coloured golden spice made from a root in the ginger family

W

Whip—to beat air into an ingredient, such as cream or egg whites, until the ingredient is light and fluffy

Whisk—a long-handled kitchen utensil with a series of wire or plastic loops at the end used to rapidly beat eggs, cream or other liquids. *Whisk* is also a verb that means 'to use a whisk'

White pepper—a spice made from the dried fruit of the pepper plant. It is more mild than black pepper

Z

Zest—a flavourful ingredient created from the outermost rind (or peel) of citrus fruits like lemons, limes and oranges. To zest a citrus fruit, ask an adult for help to find the right kitchen tool, like a zester or rasp grater. Hold the fruit over a bowl and use the zester or grater to gently scrape the outer peel, stopping when you reach the white part of the peel

Index

Page numbers in *italics* are pictures.